thoughts of a velvet heart

Bianca Nisa

thoughts of a velvet heart © 2023 Bianca Nisa

All rights reserved.

No part of this publication may be reproduced, stored in a retrieval system, or transmitted, in any form or by any means, electronic, mechanical, photocopying, recording or otherwise, without the prior written permission of the presenters.

Bianca Nisa asserts the moral right to be identified as author of this work.

Presentation by *BookLeaf Publishing*

Web: www.bookleafpub.com

E-mail: info@bookleafpub.com

ISBN: 9789357211833

First edition 2023

DEDICATION

Thank you to my parents who let me write on bathroom mirrors, and to Julia, my six-year mentor and beautiful friend who inspired my love for writing.

Overthinker

Thoughts. Thoughts. Thoughts.

A writer's overthinking melody.

Words can be a dangerous game sometimes. They form ideas, speculations, fueled by gut feeling and instinct. They keep on growing and growing until they eat you clean. Until your plate is empty.

No crumbs.

[blank page]
[white noise]
[empty room]
[lights are on but no one's home]

12:51 am

Energy level: 0

My body shuts down, my mind needs rest. My limbs are at the mercy of the wind; weightless. The foam mattress embraces me gently.

New sounds begin. Distant cars cruising the streets. Nearby dogs ending conversations. The January breeze rustling through curtains. The cool touch kissing my cheeks.

My eyes flutter like the monarch butterfly's wings in last flights. Fatigue ruminates around the warm room. Last calm breaths before I salute.

A quiet serenade to send me off.

30/08/19

My chest pulsates with feelings. My body stirs. I melt into cradling warmth while my mind imagines… what if? My heartbeat is loud in the stillness. My body trapped in desire. I wonder if another is alone in the dark, their heart aching for our embrace. Will this soul reach mine and re-connect with its missing piece? The attraction is daring, and I can't restrain. I am not falling; I am getting pulled. Not pulled by force but by what I think may be love. And I am getting pulled towards you.

Betrayal.

I could rip these pages out like grass.
Shred it. Eat it. Then spit it out like silver
bullets.
Anger burns into my face
and tears reveal hidden emotions.

I feel weak.

Say anything to me and you'd watch me crumble
into the palm of your hands. Let the wind
take me on an adventure. Somewhere far and
blissful,
with crystalline waterfalls and fairy floss skies.
Someplace
where people can feel your pain radiate and just
soothe your soul.
Someplace where honesty filters our existence.
I feel like a collectable that once felt desired,
which is now covered in a thick veil of betrayal.

My colours are fading.

April's Biggest Fool

You're scared.
You don't want to risk anything or try something new.
You have your blast while it lasts and then you ditch it.
You live in constant fear that you're going to be overpowered by someone else, when your whole life's been spent in the spotlight, being someone amazing, a 'star'.

You hate people seeing your vulnerability,
you can't stand to reveal your soul.
You're scared that if you give too much, you'll lose your shine,
that they'll leave you or hurt you instead.
You would rather break someone else's heart and watch it bleed in front of you before yours is stabbed first.

Coward.

Because why are you afraid to feel, to hurt, to be broken.
You would rather break someone else, that same someone who knows you didn't even try.

What a cruel, cruel world.

-

For a second my heart fell in synch with the
rhythm of another. It was real. Everything was
real. The tight squeeze, the smell. I shut my eyes
tight to try to preserve it as I drifted for a slight
moment where I wished for everything to be
alright. I didn't want to let go. I wanted to stay
there forever. Could I stay there forever? Please.

But as I write this, tears roll slowly down my
cheek because I know I won't have that feeling
forever, and there is nothing that I can ever do to
change that apart from endure the withdrawal
symptoms – hurt. Today made me realise that no
matter how much a person lives for another,
these feelings will never be returned. It hurts to
realise that they'll never love you back as much
as you love them.

-        one sided.

Cracked mirrors

Falling in love with an image of someone you've created inside your head freezes your heart.

They don't even exist.

And when they don't live up to be that person, you're confused. You're hurt. It's a shock to the gut. Like when you find out as a kid that Santa's a sham. Pain like when your childhood toy grows out its magic. Close pain. It tries to heal over but doesn't get the chance as the pain just keeps coming like a punch to the bruised gut in the same place over and over. Sometimes you feel like you're running in circles and you can't seem to let go since you think they'll change but you realise you're chasing clouds.

No hope.

Sometimes you need to break the circuit. Dodge the punches and attack or walk away and don't look back.

Midnights

I have nothing left. I'm trying to take comfort in soft music, to blur out the bad. I'm so hollow inside like someone's ripped out my insides. Gone. Empty.
I feel like throwing up sadness. Empty sadness. Stare at the bedroom ceiling with music blasting at night sadness. Gutted sadness. A guilt and desperate sadness. A selfish sadness. A need of a hug sadness.

~

My eyes bleed empty feelings.
I've forgotten what sleep feels like.
A hole digs its way inside me and rips every last bit of happiness. And all I'm left with is a keypad and a blank page. A place where I can let my thoughts bleed endlessly.

UNKNOWN PERSON: To be found

Why is a certain love difficult to find.

Why can't he look at me the way Ben looks at Andie Anderson. Why can't he get lost in my eyes the way Austin Ames gets lost in Sam's. Why can't he show up with flowers or even carrots like Aston Kutcher in that one film. When will he love me as much as Patrick loved Kat Stratford, where grand gestures are second nature. When will I find a man like Noah, to love me as intensely and fight with every inch of his heart until he knows he has his Allie. When will I find a love this pure it feels easy.

Is love like this even real?

：

The only thing worse than a boy who hates you
– a boy who loves you.

~ Marcus Zusak

Apologies, apologies

After a time, 'sorry' loses the value it once held.
It loses its power to mend the ashes of the heart.

I VOICED MY THOUGHTS AND
EMOTIONS AND YOU FEARED THEM.
YOU HAVE NO REASON OR RIGHT TO
HEAR THEM.

...

12

Read 10:34 am

Read 7/7/2022

'Delete conversation?'

'Delete contact?'

Empty but full

Only thing that helps with my pain is you. Blasting songs fill that void he never could. They fill me with feelings he never did. The melody plucks the pain from my heart and the curls in the lyrics make my soul feel free. Every note gently smooths a tear across my cheek and replaces my feelings of vulnerability with feelings of content.

All I've ever wanted is to love somebody as much as they love me. And now I realized I've had this the whole time. You've taught me how to love myself. You've seen me at my weakest, and you continue to build me up. I've been searching for something that's been here my whole life. I'm grateful for our friendship.

-       music

The Lucky Charm

It was like a heat wave. In it, he was a breath of
fresh air. It all came and went so quick. Felt like
the metamorphosis from stranger to friend was
compressed into a week. What I thought would
become a butterfly in the drought turned out to
be a moth.
Sparks were blown out by the universe and even
as the truth stared me blankly in the face, I still
asked, 'why?'.
The pain flooded in like prescribed medication
to the heart. One which was wearing it quite
thin.
Will I ever make it out of this current of
impracticality and torture? I keep swimming in
deep waters with my head barely above.
I'm not alone. He was slowly being strangled by
his own life, wrapped in his own problems.
When he tries to run the snakes tighten and
they'd try latch onto me. I stopped fighting to
free him as it would strangle me and turn my
heart to stone instead.
But I keep swimming with my head barely
above until I feel the sand rejoice beneath my
feet. I used to scan the beach for washed up
distractions when this whole time I've been the

lucky charm who deserves to be loved just like one.

15

DISCLAIMER: not yours

It is not my job to fix you. If you don't know yourself, it's not my job to find you. Finding yourself can take time and in the meantime we all accept the love we think we deserve.

But sometimes you don't get what you want because you deserve better.

Remember that.

:

Wanting love does not make you weak, it makes you human. That said, chasing love and partnership is different from wanting love and partnership. Words.

~ Molly Burford

Rejection? Redemption.

I was knocked down like a bowling pin.

"The work you gave me deserved a lower mark
so be happy with what you got"
"Your work is not high standard."
"Read her work, that is top marks, not yours."

STRIKE!

"You have become the most judgmental person I
know"
"Your whole personality has changed"
"You haven't stuck with a course for more than a
week."
"I don't want to be friends with the person you
have become"

DOUBLE STRIKE!!

MY SILENCE DOES NOT INDICATE
WEAKNESS. YOUR WORDS MEAN LITTLE
BUT I'VE MADE THEM INTO SOMETHING
MORE. LET MY SUCCESS BE YOUR
ANSWER.

REDEMPTION.

Her

confident yet humble
intricate but delicate
quite strikingly beautiful amongst green
and in the sun, she's truly seen
like me you see, a flower of duality

\-   The sunflower

Things that I live for

Fresh music
Salty hair and flustered sunsets
Romanians at parties
Smell of the beach on a warm night
Iced choccy milk
The truckle cheese moon
Hugs
Hot homemade bread
Gifted flowers
Watching movies tucked in bed
The rain poking the roof at 1 am
'10 Things I Hate About You'
Staring at stars
Laughing until your cheeks freeze
Speed runs with the windows down

/

We're scared of being lonely. Always seeking
comfort. Love. Security. All in a person. Our
person. It's programmed into our biology. But
look too hard and our colours will start to fade.

Those with the biggest hearts always end up
losing the most. We give so much but receive so
little. The wrong crowd will dull our energy, but
our heart will keep giving until it can't.

Oh, how will we ever learn?

~

Have faith in your journey.
Reconnect your soul with the right people.
Those who respect your love, will respect you.
Life is a blessing so stop wasting your energy on
those who don't deserve it.
Attract the energy you give.
But above all, always love with a full heart.
That's all we're ever given and all we're left
with at the very end.

22/11/22

Thank you for believing in me and trusting that I'll see it through. Thank you for teaching me to love myself and to love you. To be grateful for you. You inspire me every day, to be better and to make you proud. I cherish your spirited mind, the way you kept it young with dreams despite the passing of time. I'll try to channel those dreams and never let them go. Thank you for staying true and protecting my heart. It is soft but can be read as too extravagant and too troublesome to care for. My heart of velvet, I thank you for giving to me.

- letter to my younger self

www.ingramcontent.com/pod-product-compliance
Lightning Source LLC
LaVergne TN
LVHW050304200726
843509LV00015B/3155